LIFE IS A POEM

by
Barbara M. Appleby

Illustrations by
Brad Appleby

Published by

LIFE IS A POEM

Published in the United States of America
by Goddaughtersink.com
Available from Amazon.com
and other retail outlets.

DEDICATION

This book is dedicated to my mom.
She has been writing poems about events
in her life and those of her family for as
long as I can remember. A family tree will
help a family remember their names and dates,
but this "poetstree" will help our family
remember the events in our life together.

Thanks for the memories.
Always keep writing mom.

-Brad Appleby

SPRING

Spring is coming for you and me

Spring is coming for us to see

The pussy willow in its white fur coat swaying in the breeze

The brown bare trees will soon be covered with tiny green leaves

Ah! Smell the lovely soft spring air

That blows and goes right through your hair

The little flowers just showing their heads

Just waking out of their cold winter beds

The brown grass beginning to turn a lusty green

And listen to the robin's loud shrill scream

Once again when winter comes, and everything is cold

The robins will fly south and back, and do that 'till they are old

When winter is over once again and the pussy willows white

We can look overhead and see birds coming back in flight

For spring is here for you and me

Spring is here for us to see

THE MOVE

The winter was so very long, it never seemed to end

The snow just kept on piling up at each and every bend

Every day seemed more cold and gray

As if this winter planned to stay

We went on vacation and left our cold house

Down to Florida to visit "the mouse"

After each theme park at the end of a day

We returned to our motel in the pool to play

We did everything a tourist should do

We went everywhere, ate lots of food too

We had so much fun we hated to leave

When we got back home we became so bereaved

That same old snow we had left last week

Had been covered with more and was now really deep

We decided that moment to move away

To go to Orlando and we're here yet today

I don't miss the snow and I don't miss our house

In fact, we even work for "the mouse"

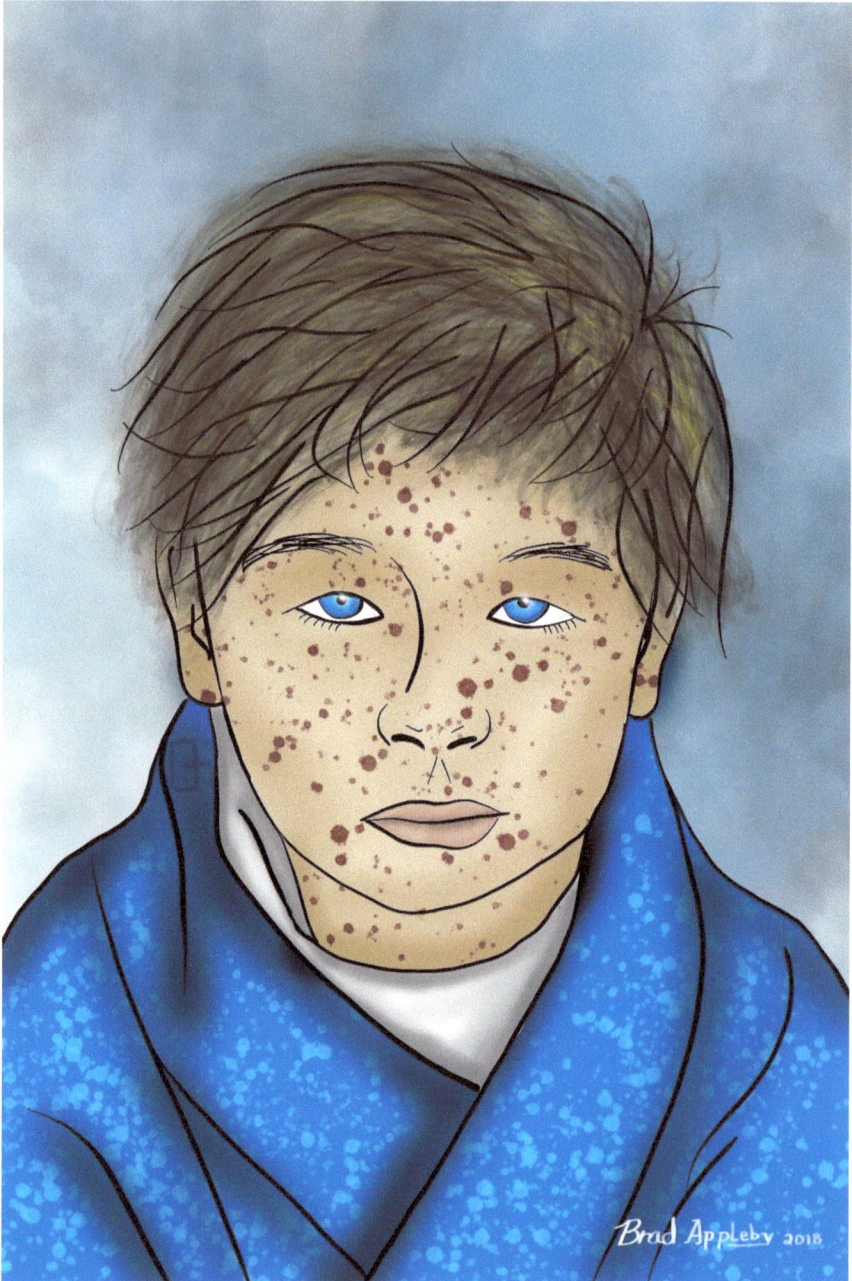

MY GRANDSON

My grandson is all chickenpox from head down to his toes

His face is red, the eyes are sore and bumps all over his nose

They seem to pop out as you watch, like weeds upon your lawn

Hopefully there will be no scars and soon it will be gone

I know this is a childhood thing, it's best to have it done

But is had seemed so much easier when they were on my son

TO CLIMB
YOUR FAMILY TREE

When I began to search my "Roots" to climb my family tree

I never dreamed what could be found how much there was to see

Each one left a paper trail for all of us to find

In churches, pictures, bibles, books, they weren't just being kind

They worked, they moved, they built a life, their children were their pride

You have to follow them you see, where ever they seemed to hide

To trace them through the years can be a wondrous trip

A captain in the army or a sailor on a ship

The time has come to get a start for all our children's sake

So they will know their family and learn the steps to take

So let's go see our relatives and write down all they say

Then we can leave behind us our paper trail today

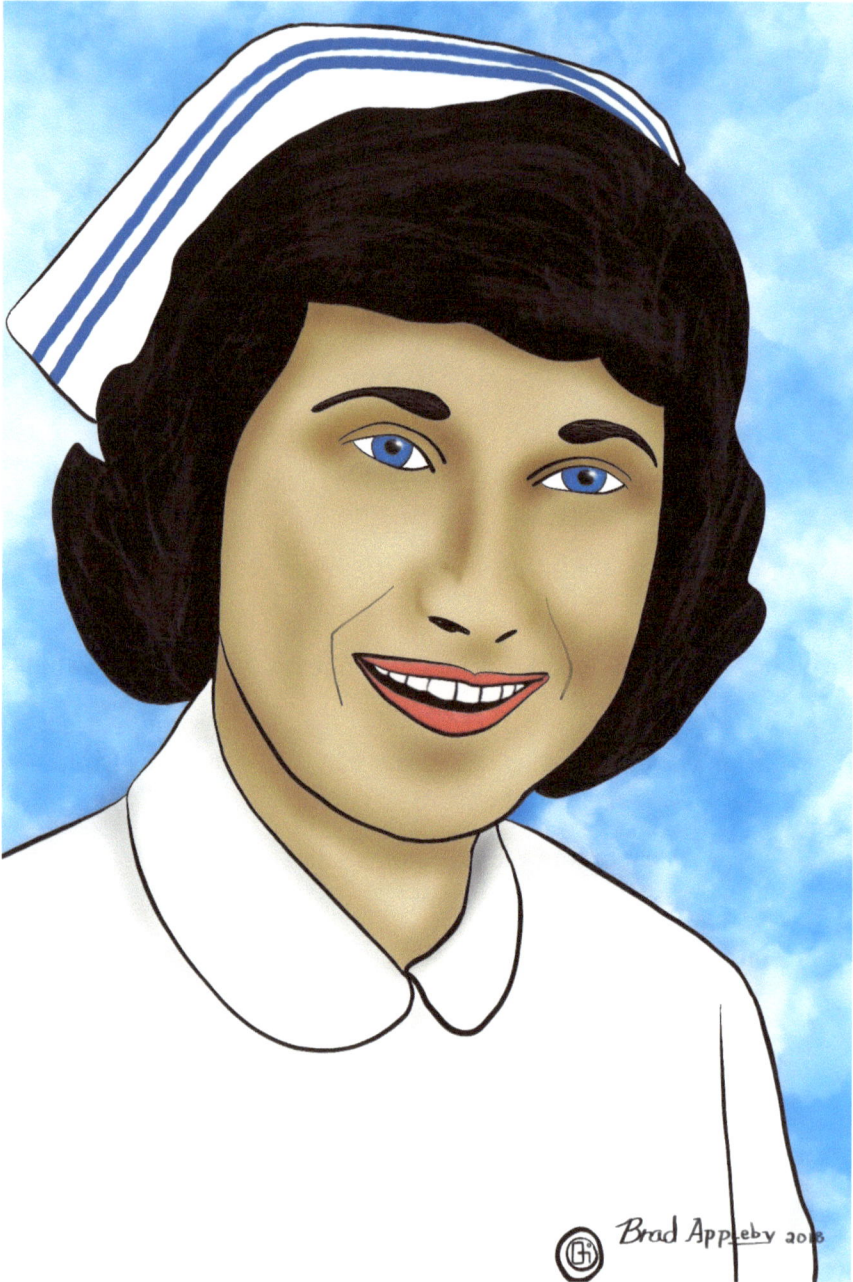

BETTER LATE THAN NEVER
MY POETRY

Why did I wait so long to write my poetry

The words just seem to flow directly out of me

When I was in school before I was a nurse

I wrote a lot of poetry, I wrote a lot of verse

Just like Grandma Moses taking up her art

It's never too late to finally make a start

MY LAUNDRY

The laundry is a boring job that never seems to end

Day by day we wash our clothes and sometimes even mend

So many times I have tried to find an easier way

So far nothing has helped me, on my laundry day

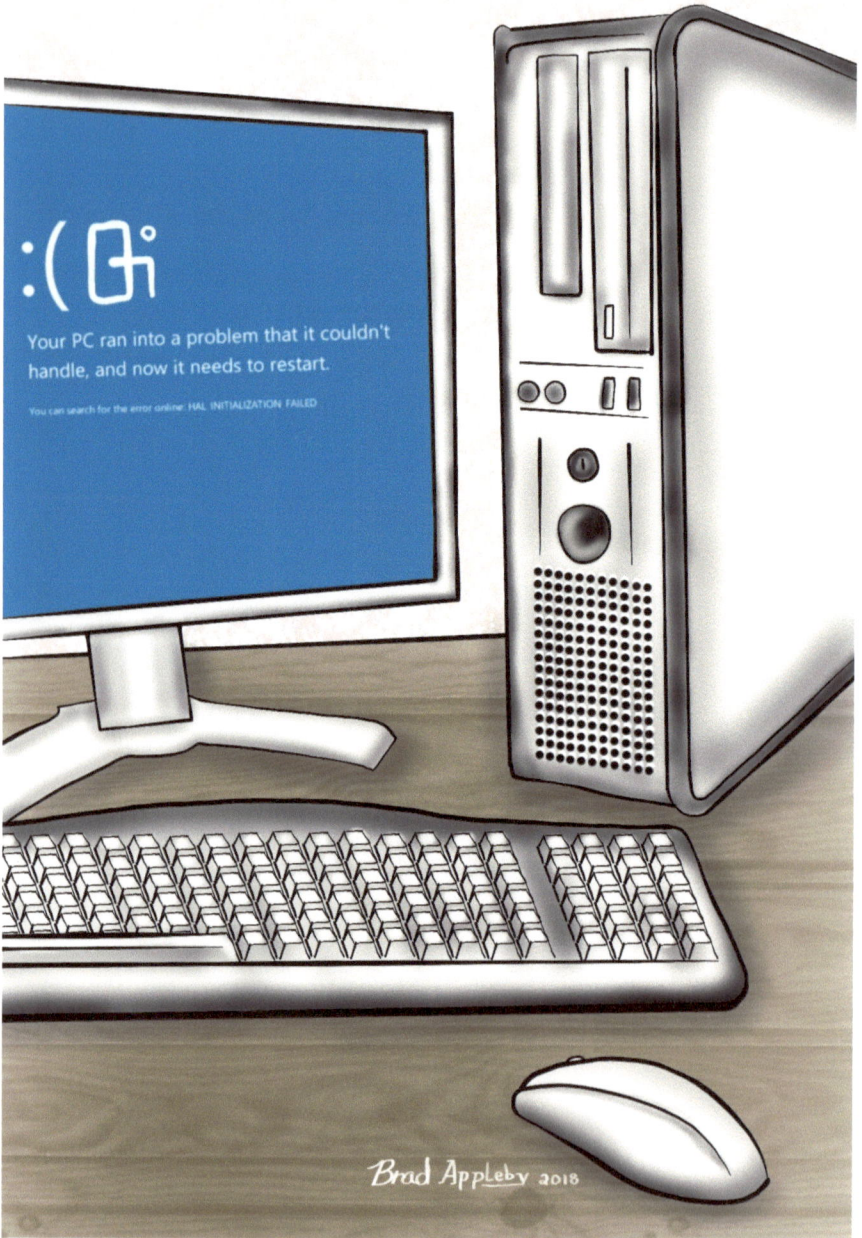

TO MY COMPUTER

I got a new computer to use every day

To organize all my bills so they would seem like play

But how in the world to use it is another tale

Hit only one wrong thing and it seems to fail

Then I sit useless staring at the keys

Wondering how to fix it shaking in my knees

I wish we had computers when I was going to school

Now I call my grandson and feel just like a fool

He doesn't seem to understand why grammy can't relate

I would guess it is because he is only eight

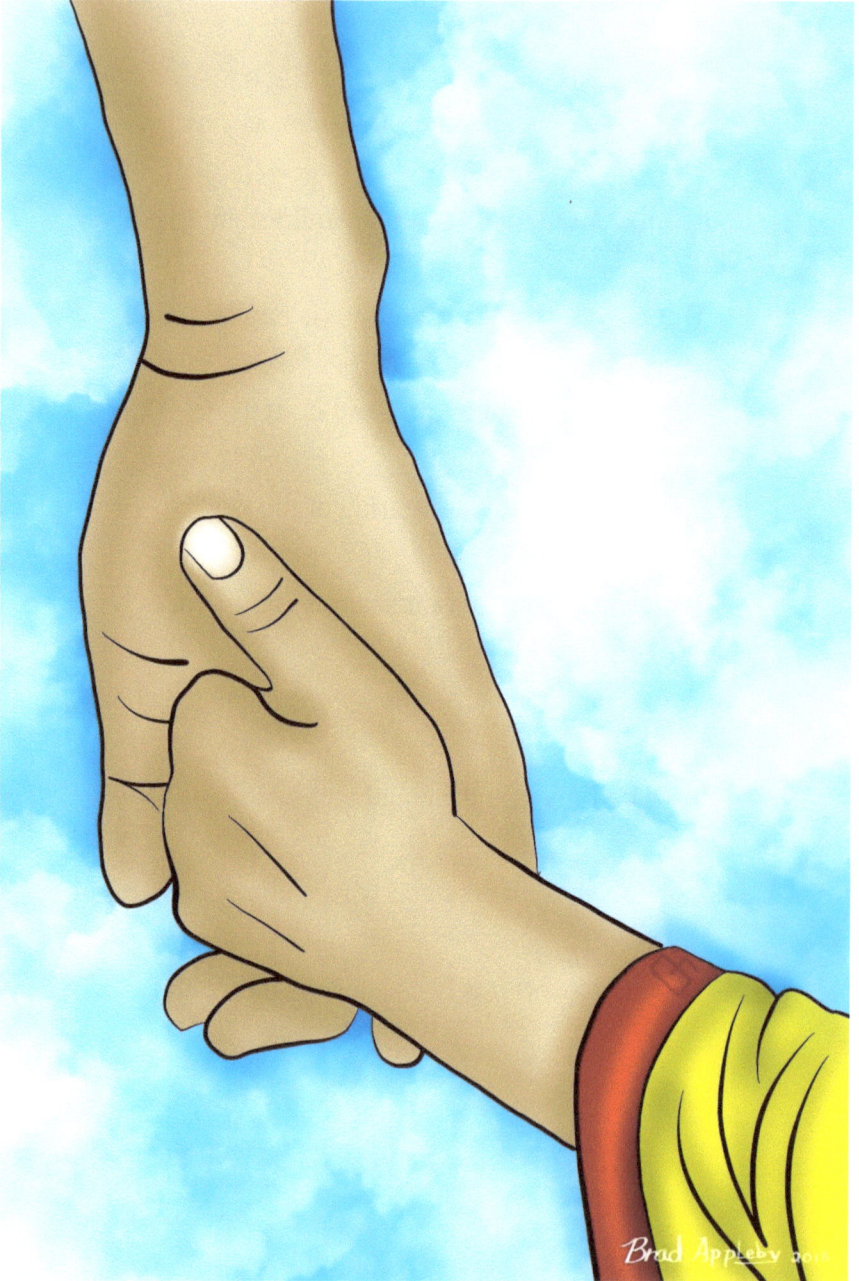

MY BABY

He leaves the nest to fly away

You hope he's ready for the day

You watched him grow into a man

You picked him up you held his hand

Over the years you did your best

It's up to him to do the rest

He's been your "Baby" and will always be

But after all he's only thirty three

A SMOKER'S LAMENT

I never thought the day would come when life would pass me by

That there would be no hope for me, that I was soon to die

How could I know the damage done each and every day

Why didn't I believe what others had to say

Now it is too late for me, my spirit has been broken

So I will die of cancer rather than quit smokin'

(In remembrance of my sister Pat)

MY CAR

It seems it always needs repairs no matter what I do

I take it in to have it checked just like they tell me to

They put it through all kinds of tests to keep it running smooth

But isn't it funny that it's never in the groove

They call you in the office and calmly close the door

And then they start to tell you it needs a whole lot more

It's that identical phrase I'm beginning now to dread

"I need to talk to you, may I go ahead?"

As I sit there listening to the amount I'll have to spend

It always makes me wonder, will it ever end

Barbara M. Appleby

CRAVINGS

I've watched my weight come and go through all these many years

If only I could keep it off it would save so many tears

But that special kind of hunger always seems to just appear

Especially when the TV's on, it seems I have to fear

It could be all those pictures of food and drink galore

Being held by skinny people who say we need some more

So I'll go to a movie and get a change of scene

But now all around me so much popcorn I could scream

There is no way to avoid it good food is here to stay

I'll have to keep my eyes shut until my hunger goes away

TO LOAN MY CAR

Why is it when I loan my car to my grown-up son

He never seems to give it back until it needs work done

The day he picked it up from me it was running well

Then I get it back and now it sounds like "hell"

There is no gas or oil which of course I just expect

But how in just two short weeks did it become a wreck

Now it needs a tune-up and a brake job too

I should have learned my lesson but moms never do

GEORGE

We had a little parakeet and George was his name

George was a special friend, he almost seemed tame

One cold winter morning we found that he had died

Bradley took it very hard and he cried and cried

Steve told his little brother "Do not be sad

George has gone to heaven instead we should be glad"

When his dad came home that day I was so inspired

So I asked Steve to tell him exactly what transpired

Slowly he started to tell that sad tale

How George had died left Steve's face so pale

"Where is George now honey, tell it like a man"

"You know, Mom you threw him in the can"

THE PLAN

The plan was very simple when our son reached seventeen

He went to join the Air Force, it was all part of his scheme

He would learn to work on airplanes and take them all apart

Then after only four years a new career he would start

Working for an airline he would then fly for free

Taking along his parents all over the world to see

It had all seemed so simple but time just seemed to fly

Instead of only four years twenty had gone by

He's now a retired "Thunderbird" enjoying each and every day

But now that he's retired his parents are too old to play

GARAGE SALES

Will you take a quarter will you take a dime

Garage sales are a lot of fun each and every time

As you're heading down the road with your paper carefully marked

Your car just seems to understand when you suddenly need to park

And then the fun begins as you get out of your car

Trying not to seem anxious even if you are

You head towards the tables and casually glance around

With so many things for sale some bargains can be found

Casually you pick some items up and pretend you really don't care

When really your only hope is that the prices will be fair

What will she want for this priceless find

You bid back and forth to reach a price you don't mind

Then it's off to your car that didn't take very long

Off to the next house before the good items are gone

OUR NEST IS EMPTY

It seemed to take so many years to empty out the nest

We thought our kids would never leave, that we would never rest

They had just seemed to come and go throughout these many years

From birth to school to college and through so many tears

First they brought home all their friends and then they brought their wives

Soon their children came along to brighten up our lives

It seems so much more difficult to get a start today

We hoped we taught them all they needed so they could move away

But now our nest is empty and we really are alone

I wonder when the kids will come or just pick up the phone

Brad Appleby 2018

THE PHOTO ALBUM

I found a photo album that my parents used to have

With all the pictures of their lives, I really was so glad

There are photos of my father in his naval uniform

When he was just a young man trying to conform

My mother was a "flapper" when she was a new bride

Smiling at the camera so full of love inside

The rest of this album is just a guess

With so many people looking their best

There are no names or dates inside so you can easily see

It isn't going to help me much add to my family tree

So let's all mark our pictures as we take them every day

With names and dates and places before we put them away

Then we will leave behind us a photo story of each day

Instead of only pictures with nothing more to say

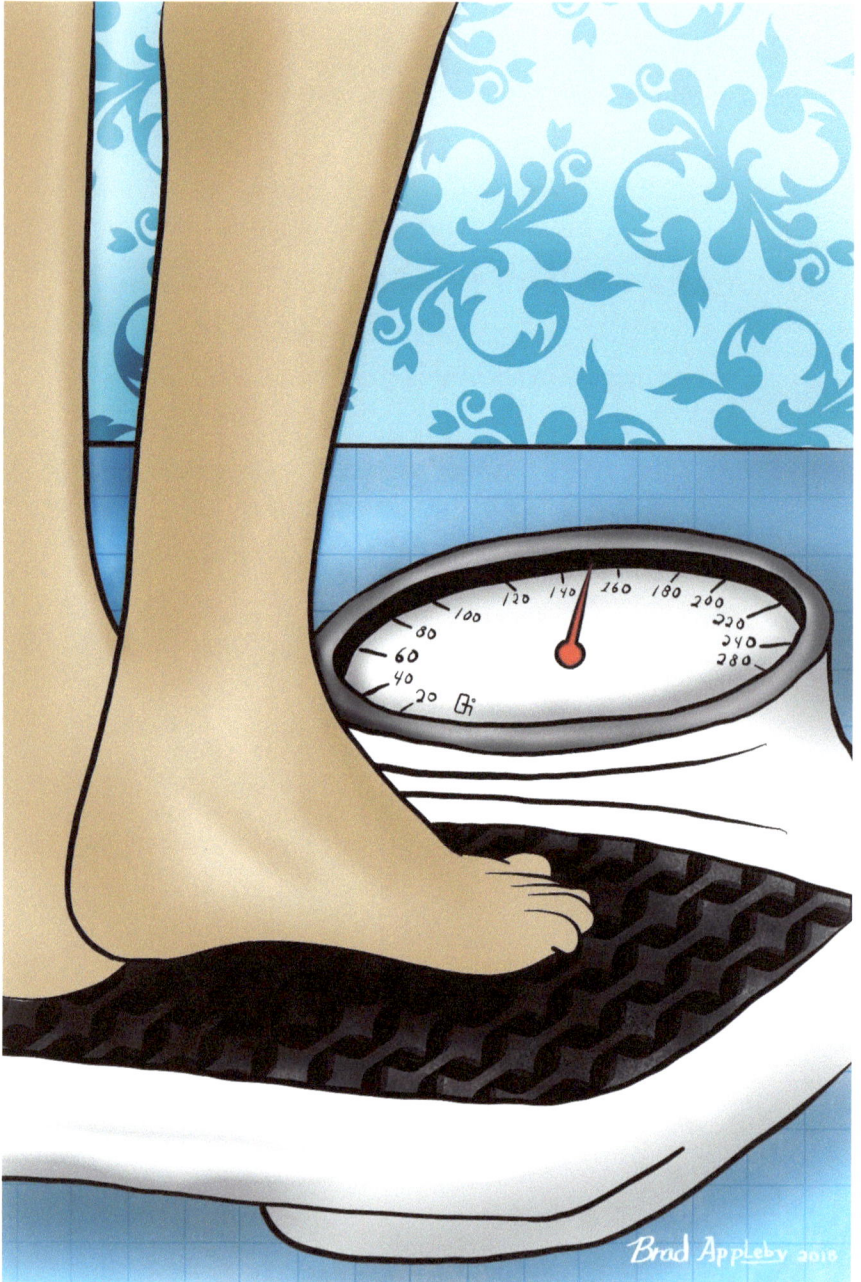

MY DIET

It all had seemed so easy to take a few pounds off

I would change my eating habits and at sweets I would scoff

So I started off so carefully and measured out my food

Each meal no fat would cross my lips, it seemed to suit my mood

The pounds would drop, my size would shrink, I would feel so alive

"Let's eat out" my husband said, too bad it was only day five

THE PROJECT

It started with a carpet that had grown too old

With places that were stained and worn and were no longer gold

My husband would replace it, but wanted tile this time

So he headed to the store to see what he could find

We now have many boxes of paint and trim and glue

But he did not realize just how hard it was to do

Just to remove the old carpet was such a big chore

It caused bloody knuckles and scratches galore

We now have a room with tile and carpet too

With boxes piled everywhere and endless work to do

When he is finally finished I will be so very glad

At least it's our last project for "Wonder Dad!"

WHEN I TURNED
THE TV OFF

When I turned the TV off I found a lot more time

I used to watch for hours each day, it really was a crime

The time that I have wasted through each and every year

Have now become a luxury and every day is dear

If only I had known this when I was very young

One can only imagine how much more I could have done

Thank goodness for that writers strike and criminal trials too

Because then I broke the habit, I don't miss it, do you

THE SKI HILL

Our teenaged sons just loved to ski

Flying down the hill for all to see

It's a good thing we lived so near the park

Where the ski hill was open even after dark

They spent all their time skiing on the snow

Going out the door each chance they could go

Down the hill they flew, the wind in their face

Enjoying the snow that flew all over the place

But there was a big problem on that ski hill one year

They came home bent and broken, on each face was a tear

It seems they had tried to ski down the hill

With only their skateboards to give them a thrill

One little thing they forgot as they flew

It was still summer and grass can be cruel

MY FAMILY TREE

As I go climbing through my "Roots" there is so much to see

There doesn't seem to be an end to climbing my family tree

It just keeps growing taller as I go up each branch

I used to think I'd finish it but I know there is no chance

So step by step I move along learning all I can

About another family with each hope and plan

My great grandfather owned a saloon along the banks of the river

And he died at age thirty-three of congestion in his liver

I had another ancestor who fought in the Civil War

Through swamps and streams he trod but never on a dry shore

How I wished I had seen my relatives as many have now passed away

What help they might have been on my journey here today

Brad Appleby 2018

LIFE IS A POEM

Have you let life pass you by

Or done those things you planned to try

Like just walk along the beach

With your loved ones in your reach

Or lying on a blanket with the night sky overhead

Picking out all the stars about which you have read

Have you taken that long hike along a nature trail

Looking at the wonders whose beauty never fails

Have you read those many books you always meant to do

Or have you never found the time to enjoy that pleasure too

This list could just go on and on as we all know it can

We need to try to take some time for things we need to plan

So let us try to have some fun each and every day

To do those things we want to do before our Poem goes away

THE ASHTRAY OF AMERICA

Have you ever looked down at the ground

To see the trash that's all around

We have become a big ashtray

Collecting more stuff every day

The cigarette butts are everywhere

Thrown around with scarcely a care

They're made so strong they will always be

Littering our grass for everyone to see

Why don't the ones that toss them away

Consider how long they will stay

Instead of just trashing their own health each day

They're trashing us too, it won't go away

Why won't they stop this terrible trashing

To keep our lands clean and green everlasting

YESTERDAY'S TOMORROW

As we journey through another year

I wonder where the time has gone

How does the time go by so fast

When yesterday's tomorrow is part of the past

So many things I had planned to do

Will have to be done in the future too

So as this year draws to an end

The only thing I can say

Is make your resolution list,

Don't wait another day

Because before you know it

This year will have passed you by

This time it wasn't just a year

But a decade that seemed to fly

IT'S A MAN THING!

They burp, they grunt they scratch their rear

You talk to them but they never hear

The remote control is in their hand

Flipping channels as fast as they can

In fact, if all the truth be known

When sports are on you're quite alone

It doesn't matter which sport they see

I think they probably would stare at a tree

With food and dishes all over the room

I can't believe it happened that soon

Then of course the real "man thing"

That all are famous for

You all know what I'm talking about

Behind that bathroom door

Why do they think that the thing to do

Is to leave that darn seat up

Why can't it just be put in place

Why can't they keep it shut

THAT SCARY DAY!

That scary day has finally come, that life might pass me by

Things had really gone so far that I could actually die

Why didn't I listen to what others had to say

About the type of food I ate each and every day

The bacon, pizza, nuts and chips were all best friends of mine

I couldn't seem to get enough, I ate them all the time

And then there was that exercise I really should have done

Almost every day, it might have seemed like fun

But no, I said, I'm doing fine just the way I am

I like my food, the way I live, can't you understand

So time for me has come and gone, and now I'm in such pain

My chest feels like it's being crushed, and oh! It's such a drain

The surgery will be starting soon, the new heart has been found

I'm so very thankful, and hope I'll stay around

It's such a wondrous thing they do, but also very sad

That someone had to lose their life, that part is really bad

I plan to lead a better life and help wherever I can

To share with all my family my new and healthy plan

I am so very thankful, that this is going to be

But how I wish I had just taken better care of me

(In remembrance of my dear friend John Logan)

THE TRUTH HURTS!

I am an old lady, my face as smooth as glass

With hardly any wrinkles, I hope that it will last

How lucky I have been to look so very good

When all my friends around me should really wear a hood

Then my sight began to go, my doctor said to me

"You need to have some surgery, to help you better see"

After it was finished both eyes were just like new

The grass and trees were beautiful, the sky so very blue

But what a shock I had that day, my heart just seemed to stop

When I looked into a mirror my mood began to drop

I couldn't believe the sight I saw, with eyes so clear to see

What happened to that face of mine, I can't believe it's me

So many lines and wrinkles had seemed to just appear

That now I know I'm really old with lines I used to fear

But even with that wrinkled face I know it's really me

I'm glad I had another chance, I would much rather see

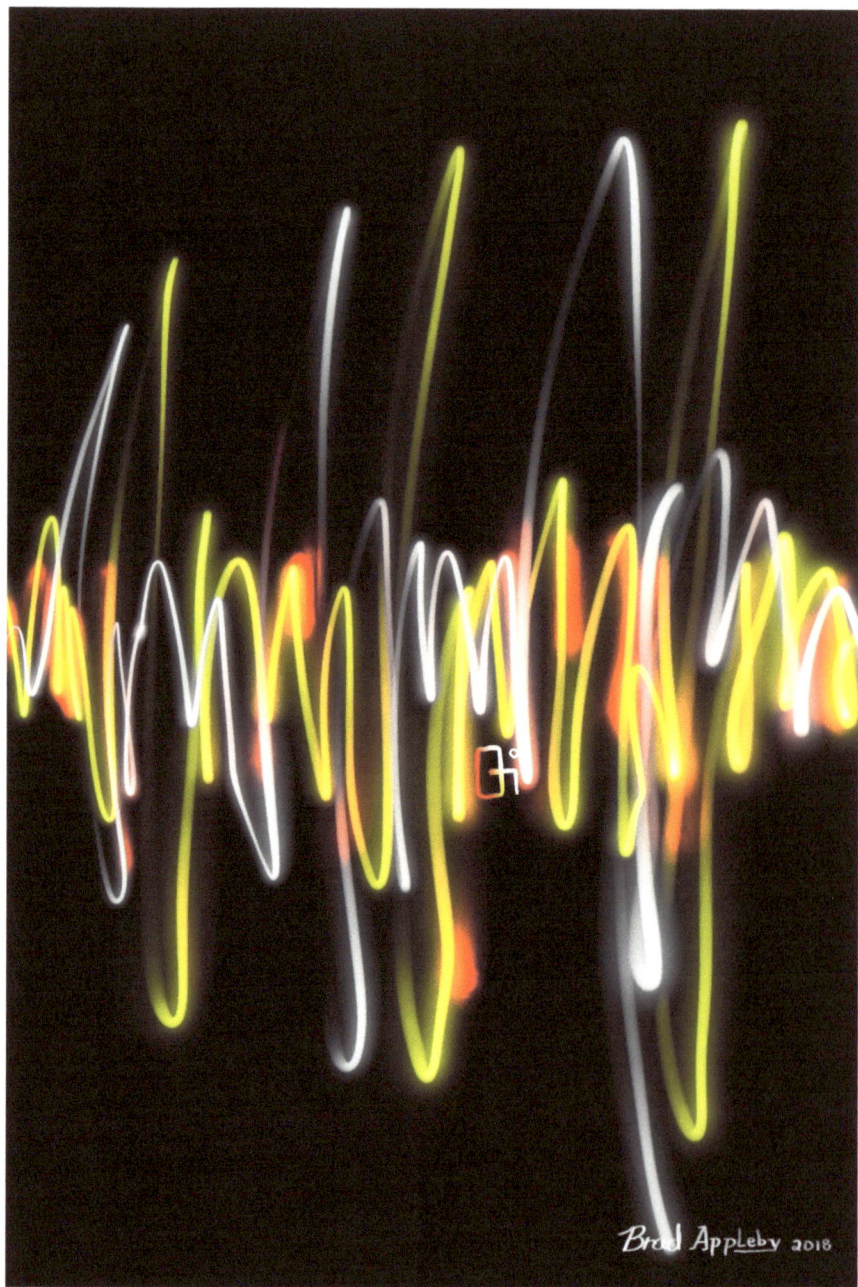

THE NOISE!

Boy was I surprised in the middle of the night

I woke up so suddenly, it gave me such a fright

I heard an awful sound in my room by my bed

It sounded so close to me, it really caused me dread

The room was so very dark, no movement I could see

But when I turned the lights on, it was only me

UNWELCOME BED PARTNER

It's the middle of the night and what do I see

A gigantic cockroach looking back at me

I felt this creature crawling on my neck

So I suddenly had to reschedule his trek

I quickly brushed him to my feet

And grabbed a flashlight to have a peek

I slammed him down to the floor

Then shot him with room spray by my door

I didn't know if this spray would be good

So I stamped on him right where he stood

Now he realized without a doubt

That this old lady has some clout

BEST MAN TOASTS

Version 1

To Steve and Amy

May you be lovers

And best friends

Putting each other before yourselves

With a love

That never ends

Version 2

To Steve and Amy

When yours and mine becomes ours

When its honey, put the kids in the car

When honey, not tonight

You're timings not right

Just remember that through it all

You've got NFL FOOTBALL

- by Steve Appleby

LOST LOVE

Love was once a word

That people kept inside

Until that special moment

When he would tell her why

Now Love is just a word

Like hello and goodbye

Said without the feeling felt deep inside

- by Brad Appleby

Barbara M. Appleby

I JUST SWALLOWED A CHERRY PIT!

I just swallowed a cherry pit!

I don't know how well it will sit.

I swallowed it on a dare

Because I really don't care

To have my friends think I'm a coward.

I just swallowed a cherry pit!

And I didn't like it one bit.

My parents tried to comfort me,

By saying it will only grow into a tree!

Trust me, that seriously didn't help.

I just swallowed a cherry pit!

I wish I had my baseball mitt.

It really is such a bore,

So much that I actually snore,

Wondering if I'm going to be okay.

I just swallowed a cherry pit!

I want to have my stomach lit.

My friend who loves berries

And also loves cherries

Wished she were in my place.

I just swallowed a cherry pit!

However, my friend Kit

Says to look on the positive side.

But I really can't abide

Even if I *do* get to eat cherries whenever I want.

I just swallowed a cherry pit!

And when my grave says R.I.T.,

I'll still have that thing inside me.

Unless we get it out, you see,

I'll have it in forever!

- by Sophia Zhong

MOTHER EARTH

Elephants, zebras
Big and small
Mother Earth
Made us all

We, the smartest
Must follow her will
We, the strongest
Must try not to kill

She looks down upon us
A frown, she's sad
Help her now
Don't make her mad

She must wait and wait
For us to change
Reward her now
Let her rate

Who we really are

- by Sophia Zhong